Lakewood Memorial Free Library

IN MEMORY OF

Eric Carl Westrom

———•———

PRESENTED BY

Mr. & Mrs. Burton M. Anderson

Poetry for Spring

Selected by Lillie Patterson

Drawings by Kelly Oechsli

GARRARD PUBLISHING COMPANY
CHAMPAIGN, ILLINOIS

Library of Congress Cataloging in Publication Data
Patterson, Lillie, comp.
  Poetry for spring.
  (Reading shelf-poetry)
  SUMMARY: Poems by various poets describe the
advent, activities, sights, and holidays of spring.
  1. Spring—Juvenile poetry. [1. Spring—Poetry]
I. Oechsli, Kelly, illus. II. Title.
PZ8.3.P2736Po   808.81   73–3186
ISBN 0–8116–4114–7

The editor and publisher acknowledge with thanks permission
received to reprint the poems in this collection.

Acknowledgments and formal notices of copyright for all
material under copyright appear on pages 61 and 62, which are
hereby made an extension of the copyright page.

Contents

Spring

I'm shouting
I'm singing
I'm swinging through trees
I'm winging skyhigh
With the buzzing black bees.
I'm the sun
I'm the moon
I'm the dew on the rose.
I'm a rabbit
Whose habit
Is twitching his nose.
I'm lively
I'm lovely
I'm kicking my heels.
I'm crying "Come dance"
To the fresh water eels.
I'm racing through meadows
Without any coat
I'm a gamboling lamb
I'm a light leaping goat
I'm a bud
I'm a bloom
I'm a dove on the wing.
I'm running on rooftops
And welcoming spring!

Karla Kuskin

News of Spring

A dandelion stood tall and yellow,
Spreading the news like a gay young fellow;
And he nodded the word—
"It's spring!"

A robin said that a breeze he knew
Had brought him the message,
And it was true;
And the robin twittered—
"It's spring!"

A cherry blossom unfolded white
As popping corn, on a bough last night;
And waved us below—
"It's spring!"

And we looked at the sky
And the tree
And the ground,
And there—sure enough—
It was spring
All around!

Dorothy Brown Thompson

In the Garden

It's good to be back
    At the soil again,
Out in the garden
    To toil again.

It's good to plant
    And to sow again,
To dig and to rake
    And to hoe again.

I'm happy and merry:
    I sing again,
Because today
    It is spring again.

Ilo Orleans

For, lo, the winter is past,
The rain is over and gone;
The flowers appear on the earth;
The time of the singing of birds is come. . . .

From The Bible
Song of Solomon 2:11-12

Spring

Everyone's bursting outdoors, outdoors,
Oh, nobody can stay in;
For now is the moment to oil your skates
Or bring out a top to spin;
To find marbles or jacks or a skipping rope,
To tape up a baseball bat,
Or decide on a circus,
Charge a pin,
And *I'll* be the acrobat!

Dorothy Aldis

Take Me Out to the Ball Game

Take me out to the ball game
Take me out with the crowd
Buy me some peanuts and crackerjack
I don't care if I never get back
Let me root, root, root for the home team
If they don't win it's a shame
For it's one, two, three strikes you're out
At the old ball game.

Jack Norworth

Kite Song

I am a kite high in the sky,
Floating along with the wind,
And the funniest thing . . .
I'm holding a string,
With a boy on the other end!

Avan Collum

Kite Days

A kite, a sky, and a good firm breeze,
And acres of ground away from trees,
And one hundred yards of clean, strong string,
O boy, O boy! I call that spring.

Mark Sawyer

Maple Feast

Into the bit-flaked sugar-snow
The crystal-gathering sledges go.

Stumbling through silver to my knees,
I shout among the maple trees,

Tilt gleaming buckets icy cold
Till I am full as I can hold

Of clear bright sap, until I feel
Like a maple tree from head to heel!

Then to the sugarhouse I run
Where syrup, golden as the sun,

Is boiling in the crisp March air
And I, as daft as a baby bear,

Eat, till my buttons burst asunder
From maple sweetness, maple wonder!

Frances Frost

Wind Song

When the wind blows
the quiet things speak.
Some whisper, some clang,
some creak.

Grasses swish.
Treetops sigh.
Flags slap
and snap at the sky.
Wires on poles
whistle and hum.
Ashcans roll.
Windows drum.

When the wind goes—
suddenly
then,
the quiet things
are quiet again.

Lilian Moore

The March Wind

I come to work as well as play;
  I'll tell you what I do;
I whistle all the live-long day,
  "Woo-oo-oo-oo! Woo-oo!"

I toss the branches up and down
  And shake them to and fro,
I whirl the leaves in flocks of brown,
  And send them high and low.

I strew the twigs upon the ground,
  The frozen earth I sweep;
I blow the children round and round
  And wake the flowers from sleep.

Unknown

17

Wind Capers

He is huffing,
Puff-puff puffing,
He is chuffing
And he's bluffing,
He is running rampant,
Roaring up and down.

He is blowing
For he's knowing
That the snowing
Will be going,
And he's cutting capers
Like a circus clown.

Things are peeping
That were sleeping,
Things are creeping
And he's sweeping
All the dust and drabness
That he finds in town.

Lillie Patterson

Letter to a Robin in March

Dear robin who has gone away
From snow and icy rain,
We hope you'll soon be coming back
To visit us again.

We've written to the flowers,
The peach tree, and the plum,
To ask *them* back, and all of them
Said they'd be *glad* to come.

Kathryn Worth

March

In the maple-sugar bush
When the first sap flows,
The air has the sweetness
Of the chill melting snows,
And the March breezes sound
To the clamor of the crows.

Not a flower blossoms yet,
Not a leaf is unfurled,
The bear lies asleep
In his deep cavern curled,
And a dappled sky hangs
O'er a snow-dappled world.

Now the Indian ghosts,
Single file, return
When the maple sap runs
And the sugar fires burn . . .
What was that which stirred the thicket?
What footstep moved the fern?

Elizabeth Coatsworth

Go Wind

Go wind, blow
Push wind, swoosh.
    Shake things
    take things
    make things
       fly.

    Ring things
    swing things
    fling things
       high.

Go wind, blow
Push things—whee.
    No, wind, no.
    Not me—
    not *me*.

       Lilian Moore

The Wind

I heard the wind blow.
I saw the wind blow.
    It whistled,
    It whirred,
    It whirled.

The branches crackled.
The green leaves shook,
    And twisted,
    And trembled,
    And curled.

The wind blew loud.
The wind blew long.
    It rumbled,
    It thundered,
    It roared.

The great trees swayed.
The sky grew black,
    And it rained,
    And it stormed,
    And it poured.

Ilo Orleans

From . . .

March

Dear March, come in!
How glad I am!
I looked for you before.
Put down your hat—
You must have walked—
How out of breath you are!
Dear March, how are you?
And the rest?
Did you leave Nature well?
Oh, March, come right upstairs with me,
I have so much to tell.

Emily Dickinson

I'll Wear a Shamrock

St. Patrick's day is with us,
The day when all that's seen
To right and left and everywhere
Is green, green, green!

And Irish tunes they whistle
And Irish songs they sing,
Today each Irish lad walks out
As proud as any king.

I'll wear an Irish shamrock
In my coat, the glad day through,
For my father and mother are Irish
And I am Irish, too!

Mary Carolyn Davies

Leprechaun Song

I saw a man,
A teeny-tiny man,
'Twas a leprechaun, I know.
He hammered and he tapped
and he sang a song
and his shoes were in a row.

"Oh!
Never a lump,
Never a bump,
Never a pinch-a-toe.
I make my shoes
with a tap-tap-tap
and a tic-tac-tic-tac-toe.
Oh!"

Ida DeLage

In Time of Silver Rain

In time of silver rain
The earth
Puts forth new life again,
Green grasses grow
And flowers lift their heads,
And over all the plain
The wonder spreads
    Of life,
    Of life,
    Of life!

In time of silver rain
The butterflies
Lift silken wings
To catch a rainbow cry,
And trees put forth
New leaves to sing
In joy beneath the sky
As down the roadway
Passing boys and girls
Go singing, too,
In time of silver rain
    When spring
    And life
    Are new.

Langston Hughes

April Song

April is made of
such wonderful things:
    Sunbeams and tulips
and butterfly wings,

Cherry-tree blossoms
and little green shoots,
    Umbrellas and puddles
and red rubber boots,

Lambs in the meadows
and children in swings;
    April is made of
such wonderful things!

Ruth Adams Murray

Rain in April

Rain has such fun in April,
    It patters through the trees,
Talking to all the leaf buds
    And robins that it sees.

It splashes in the puddles
    And skips upon the walks,
Goes coasting down the grass blades
    And dandelion stalks.

It dips in all the flowers
    And when the clouds go by
It paints with flower colors
    A rainbow in the sky!

Eleanor Hammond

Rainbow for Joyce

Once in a while,
In a bright spring sky,
A sprinkly, sparkly, rain goes by.
And the sunbeams shine
Through the raindrops clear,
To make a magical bridge appear.
From meadow to hill
In a great wide sweep,
The magical colors begin to peep.
Yellow and green,
Violet and blue,
Orange and red come shining through.

Oh lovely rainbow,
Why can't you stay?
Like all things lovely,
You fade away.
I think I know what I will do,
For I know a magical trick or two.
I'll pluck your jewels,
So bright and gay,
And tuck them down in my heart today.
And there they will forever stay,
To shimmer and glow
When skies are grey.

Ida DeLage

April Rain Song

Let the rain kiss you.
Let the rain beat upon your head with silver liquid drops.
Let the rain sing you a lullaby.

The rain makes still pools on the sidewalk.
The rain makes running pools in the gutter.
The rain plays a little sleep-song on our roof at night—

And I love the rain.

Langston Hughes

City Rain

Rain in the city!
    I love to see it fall
Slantwise where the buildings crowd
    Red brick and all.
Streets of shiny wetness
    Where the taxis go,
With people and umbrellas all
    Bobbing to and fro.

Rain in the city!
    I love to hear it drip
When I am cosy in my room
    Snug as any ship,
With toys spread on the table,
    With a picture book or two,
And the rain like a rumbling tune that sings
    Through everything I do.

Rachel Field

Umbrellas

When the rain is raining
    And April days are cool
All the big umbrellas
    Go bumping home from school.
They bump the blowing cloudburst,
    They push the pushing storm.
They leap a muddy puddle
Or get into a huddle
    To keep each other warm.

But who is underneath them
    You really cannot tell
Unless you know the overshoes
    Or rubbers very well
Or the flippy-flop galoshes
With their swishes and their swashes
Or the running rubber boots
With their scampers and their scoots . . .

Oh, when the rain is raining
    And April days are cool
I like to watch umbrellas
    Come bumping home from school!
I like to watch and wonder
Who's hiding halfway under . . .

Rowena Bennett

The Rain

The rain came down in torrents
    And Mary said, "Oh! dear,
I'll have to wear my waterproof,
    And rubbers too, I fear."

So carefully protected—
    She started off to school
When the big round sun
    Came out and chuckled—
      "April Fool."

Unknown

From . . .

April

So here we are in April, in showy, blowy April,
In frowsy, blowsy April, the rowdy, dowdy time;
In soppy, sloppy April, in wheezy, breezy April,
In ringing, stinging April, with a singing swinging rhyme!

So here we are in April, in tipsy, gypsy April,
In showery, flowery April, the twinkly, sprinkly days;
In tingly, jingly April, in highly wily April,
In mighty, flighty April with its highty-tighty ways!

Ted Robinson

Sing-Time

Robin, sing to the rainbow!
Song-thrush, sing to the blue!
Springtime is on the hilltops
And all the world is new!

Winter slipped out through the valley
Where the pink and purple haze is;
And here is April with her arms
A-brimming full of daisies!

Rose Waldo

Rain Sizes

Rain comes in various sizes.
Some rain is as small as a mist.
It tickles your face with surprises,
And tingles as if you'd been kissed.

Some rain is the size of a sprinkle
And doesn't put out all the sun.
You can see the drops sparkle and twinkle,
And a rainbow comes out when it's done.

Some rain is as big as a nickle
And comes with a crash and a hiss.
It comes down too heavy to tickle.
It's more like a splash than a kiss.

When it rains the right size and you're wrapped in
Your rainclothes, it's fun out of doors.
But run home before you get trapped in
The big rain that rattles and roars.

John Ciardi

Easter Eggs

Humpty Dumpty has country cousins
Who come to the city in Spring by dozens;
They make such a brilliant show in town
You'd think that a rainbow had tumbled down.
Blue and yellow and pink and green,
The gayest gowns that ever were seen.
Purple and gold and oh! such style;
They are all the rage for a little while
But their visit is short for no one stays
After the Easter holidays.

Unknown

The Easter Rabbit

The Easter Rabbit keeps a very
Cheerful hen that likes to lay
Blue and red and green and yellow
Eggs for him on Easter day.

He puts the eggs inside his basket
With a lot of other things—
Bunnies with pink ears and whiskers,
Little ducks with tickling wings.

Then on tiptoe he comes hopping,
Hiding secrets everywhere—
Speckled eggs behind the mirror,
Sugar bird-nests in the chair.

If we saw him we would give him
Tender lettuce leaves to eat—
But he slips out very softly
On his pussywillow feet.

Dorothy Aldis

Passover
(The Festival of Freedom)

The Festival of Freedom
comes happily in spring—
freedom for a people,
and every growing thing;

Freedom from a bitter
bondage long ago,
freedom from the bondage
of winter's cold and snow.

Aileen Fisher

First Night of Passover

Only unleavened bread this night—
for Moses cried, "Move fast!
We cannot wait for bread to rise.
We leave this land . . . at last."

Only the bitter herbs this night—
to symbolize the years
we had no rights in Egypt land,
just work and sweat and tears.

But comfort in our chairs tonight,
now life is free and good,
and we begin the Pesach feast
with joy and gratitude!

Aileen Fisher

May Song

Spring is coming, spring is coming,
Birdies, build your nest;
Weave together straw and feather,
Doing each your best.

Spring is coming, spring is coming,
Flowers are coming too;
Pansies, lilies, daffodillies,
Now are coming through.

Spring is coming, spring is coming,
All around is fair;
Shimmer and quiver on the river,
Joy is everywhere.

Old Country Rhyme

If We're Lucky

Early in the month of May
Orioles are on their way
To stay the summer through.

And this is what we've learned to do:
Cut some oranges in two,
Hang these on a bush or tree
And wait and see . . .

And if we're lucky, there he is
Orange as the oranges—
The first to guzzle with his bill,
Drink his greedy little fill.

When he's finished, hard to say
Did bird or orange
Fly away?

Dorothy Aldis

From . . .

The Maypole Dance

A rainbow of colorful ribbons
Brightens the playground today
A maypole encircled with garlands
Welcomes the first day of May
For it's Maying time, and playing time
It's skipping time, and tripping time
Heigh-hay for Merry May Day!

It's round and round, and up and down
As dancers twirl to timing
It's in and out, and turn about
The maypole streamers twining
For it's spring time, and sing time
It's May time, holiday time
Heigh-hay for Merry May Day!

Lillie Patterson

Maytime Magic

A little seed
For me to sow . . .

A little earth
To make it grow . . .
A little hole,
A little pat . . .
A little wish,
And that is that.

A little sun,
A little shower . . .
A little while,
And then—a flower!

Mabel Watts

May Morning

May mornings are merry,
May mornings are gay,
For every green hedgerow
Is fragrant with May,
And every blithe blackbird
Is singing like mad,
And nothing is dreary
Or weary or sad.
The sun's warm and friendly,
The breeze soft and cool,
And gay little children
Go dancing to school.

Ivy O. Eastwick

That May Morning

That May morning—very early—
As I walked the city street,
Not a single store was open
Any customer to greet.

That May morning—it was early—
As I walked the avenue,
I could stop and stare and
    window-shop,
And hear the pigeons coo.

Early, early that May morning
I could skip and jump and run
And make shadows on the
    sidewalk,
Not disturbing anyone.

All the windows, all the lamp posts,
Every leaf on every tree
That was growing through the
    sidewalk
Seemed to be there just for me.

Leland B. Jacobs

Arbor Day

Let's plant a patch of purple shade,
a harp for winds to play,

Let's plant a perch where birds can rest
or hide a nest away.

Let's plant a secret place to climb,
a golden fall bouquet,

Let's plant a pile of leaves to scuff . . .
let's plant a tree today!

Aileen Fisher

From . . .

Planting a Tree

Firm in the good brown earth
Set we our little tree.
Clear dews will freshen it,
Cool rain will feed it,
Sun will be warming it
As warmth is needed.
Winds will blow round it free—
Take root, good tree!

Nancy Byrd Turner

Trees

Trees are the kindest things I know,
They do no harm, they simply grow

And spread a shade for sleepy cows,
And gather birds among their boughs.

They give us fruit in leaves above,
And wood to make our houses of,

And leaves to burn on Hallowe'en,
And in the Spring new buds of green.

They are the first when day's begun
To touch the beams of morning sun,

They are the last to hold the light
When evening changes into night,

And when a moon floats on the sky
They hum a drowsy lullaby

Of sleepy children long ago . . .
Trees are the kindest things I know.

Harry Behn

City Trees

The trees along this city street,
    Save for the traffic and the trains,
Would make a sound as thin and sweet
    As trees in country lanes.

And people standing in their shade
    Out of a shower, undoubtedly
Would hear such music as is made
    Upon a country tree.

Oh, little leaves that are so dumb
    Against the shrieking city air,
I watch you when the wind has come,—
    I know what sound is there.

              Edna St. Vincent Millay

What Do We Plant?

What do we plant when we plant the tree?
We plant the ship, which will cross the sea.
We plant the mast to carry the sails;
We plant the planks to withstand the gales—
The keel, the keelson, and beam and knee;
We plant the ship when we plant the tree.

What do we plant when we plant the tree?
We plant the houses for you and me.
We plant the rafters, the shingles, the floors,
We plant the studding, the lath, the doors,
The beams and siding, all parts that be;
We plant the house when we plant the tree.

What do we plant when we plant the tree?
A thousand things that we daily see;
We plant the spire that out-towers the crag,
We plant the staff for our country's flag,
We plant the shade, from the hot sun free;
We plant all these when we plant the tree.

Henry Abbey

A Spike of Green

When I went out
The sun was hot,
It shone upon
My flower pot.

And there I saw
A spike of green
That no one else
Had ever seen—

On other days
The things I see
Are mostly old
Except for me.

But this green spike
So new and small
Had never yet
Been seen at all!

Barbara Baker

Only One Mother

Hundreds of stars in the pretty sky,
　　Hundreds of shells on the shore together,
Hundreds of birds that go singing by,
　　Hundreds of lambs in the sunny weather.

Hundreds of dewdrops to greet the dawn,
　　Hundreds of bees in the purple clover,
Hundreds of butterflies on the lawn,
　　But only one mother the wide world over.

George Cooper

On Mother's Day

On Mother's Day we got up first,
so full of plans we almost burst.

We started breakfast right away
as our surprise for Mother's Day.

We picked some flowers, then hurried back
to make the coffee—rather black.

We wrapped our gifts and wrote a card
and boiled the eggs—a little hard.

And then we sang a serenade,
which burned the toast, I am afraid.

But mother said, amidst our cheers,
"Oh, what a big surprise, my dears.
I've not had such a treat in years."
And she was smiling to her ears!

Aileen Fisher

Jim

There never was a nicer boy
Than Mrs. Jackson's Jim.
The sun should drop its greatest gold
On him.
Because, when Mother-dear was sick,
He brought her cocoa in.
And brought her broth, and brought her bread.
And brought her medicine.
And, tipping, tidied up her room.
And would not let her see
He missed his game of baseball
Terribly.

Gwendolyn Brooks

Night and Morning

The morning sits outside afraid
Until my mother draws the shade;

Then it bursts in like a ball,
Splashing sun all up the wall.

And the evening is not night
Until she's tucked me in just right
And kissed me and turned off the light.

Oh, if my mother went away
Who would start the night and day?

Dorothy Aldis

The Sign

Summer is near
How do I know?
Why, this very day
A robin sat on a tilting spray
And merrily sang a song of May.

Unknown

Acknowledgments

Appleton-Century-Crofts: For "What Do We Plant?" by Henry Abbey, from *The Poems of Henry Abbey* published by D. Appleton and Company, 1904. Reprinted by permission of Appleton-Century-Crofts.

Atheneum Publishers, Inc.: For "Wind Song" and "Go Wind" by Lilian Moore from *I Feel The Same Way*. Text copyright © 1967 by Lilian Moore. Used by permission of Atheneum Publishers.

Rowena Bennett: For "Umbrellas" by Rowena Bennett. Reprinted from *Story-Teller Poems*, copyright 1948, by permission of the author.

Child Life: For "Kite Song" by Avan Collum from *Child Life*, copyright © 1959 by Child Life, Inc. Reprinted by permission of Child Life.

Thomas Y. Crowell Company: For "Arbor Day," "First Night of Passover," "Passover," and "On Mother's Day" from *Skip Around the Year* by Aileen Fisher, Copyright © 1967 by Aileen Fisher. With permission of the publisher, Thomas Y. Crowell Company, Inc. For "A Spike of Green" by Barbara Baker from *Shoots of Green* by Ella Bramblett, Copyright © 1968 by Ella Bramblett. With permission of Thomas Y. Crowell Company, Inc., publisher.

Ida DeLage: For "Rainbow for Joyce" and "Leprechaun Song." Reprinted by permission of the author, who controls all rights. Copyright © 1973.

Eleanor H. Doar: For "Rain in April" by Eleanor Hammond. Copyright 1926, 1954, by Rand McNally & Company. Reprinted by permission of Eleanor H. Doar.

Doubleday & Company, Inc.: For "City Rain" from the book *Taxis and Toadstools* by Rachel Field, copyright 1926 by Doubleday & Company, Inc. Reprinted by permission.

Ivy O. Eastwick: For "May Morning" by Ivy O. Eastwick. From *Jack and Jill* Magazine, 1947, published by Curtis Publishing Company. Reprinted by permission of the author, who controls all rights.

Norma Millay Ellis: For "City Trees" by Edna St. Vincent Millay from *Collected Poems*, Harper & Row. Copyright 1921, 1948 by Edna St. Vincent Millay. Reprinted by permission of Norma Millay Ellis.

Harcourt Brace Jovanovich, Inc.: For "Trees" by Harry Behn. From *The Little Hill*, copyright 1949, by Harry Behn. Reprinted by permission of Harcourt Brace Jovanovich, Inc.

Harper & Row, Publishers, Inc.: For "Spring" from *In the Middle of the Trees* by Karla Kuskin. Copyright © 1958 by Karla Kuskin. For "Jim" from *Bronzeville Boys and Girls* by Gwendolyn Brooks. Copyright © 1956 by Gwendolyn Brooks Blakely. Reprinted by permission of Harper & Row, Publishers, Inc.

Holt, Rinehart and Winston, Inc.: For "That May Morning" from *Is Somewhere Always Far Away* by Leland B. Jacobs. Copyright © 1967 by Leland B. Jacobs. Reprinted by permission of Holt, Rinehart and Winston, Inc.

Freide Orleans Joffe: For "In the Garden" by Ilo Orleans from *Rainbow in the Sky* by Louis Untermeyer and "The Wind" by Ilo Orleans from *I Watch the World Go By* by Ilo Orleans, published by Henry Z. Walck, Inc., 1961. By permission of Freide Orleans Joffe.

Index of Authors